Delightfully Disturbing Lists About the Paranormal and Unexplained

Heather E. Schwartz

CAPSTONE PRESS
a capstone imprint

Published by Capstone Press, an imprint of Capstone
1710 Roe Crest Drive, North Mankato, Minnesota 56003
capstonepub.com

Copyright © 2026 by Capstone. All rights reserved. No part of this publication may be reproduced in whole or in part, or stored in a retrieval system, or transmitted in any form or by any means, electronic, mechanical, photocopying, recording, or otherwise, without written permission of the publisher.

Library of Congress Cataloging-in-Publication Data is available on the Library of Congress website.

ISBN: 9798875228278 (hardcover)
ISBN: 9798875232015 (paperback)
ISBN: 9798875232022 (ebook PDF)

Summary: Spooky season can be all year long when the scariest, most spine-tingling facts about the paranormal are collected in this book of delightfully disturbing lists. Chapters make the content event more digestible. Full-color images and inviting designs will engage readers' minds and get them excited to learn more.

Editorial Credits
Editor: Marissa Bolte; Designer: Kay Fraser;
Media Researcher: Svetlana Zhurkin;
Production Specialist: Katy LaVigne

Image Credits
Alamy: Jason O. Watson (USA: California photographs), 11; Capstone: Kay Fraser (design elements), cover and throughout; Getty Images: BrendanHunter, 26, Fotokita, cover (ghost), Joe_Potato, cover (doll), ronib1979, cover (UFO), Yelena Babenkova, cover (Loch Ness Monster); Shutterstock: Aalana, 14, adike, cover (alien), 20, art of line, 31, cornfield, 28, Daniel Eskridge, 16, 17, DanieleGay, 25, Donato Fierro Perez, 27, Elena Korobeynikova, 6, Everett Collection, 30, Gregory M. Davis Jr, 18, Irina Senkova, cover (skulls), Kirk Gulden, cover (Alcatraz), kittirat roekburi, 5, Mikadun, 21, Naeblys, 24, Nagel Photography, 22, Navigator-tour, 12, New Africa, 29, Oliver Denker, 13, Paul Juser, 19, Pauline Fox, 9, PongMoji, 10, Sean Pavone, 7, Sergey Uryadnikov, 15, sezer66, 8, Victoria OM, 4, Wirestock Creators, 23

Any additional websites and resources referenced in this book are not maintained, authorized, or sponsored by Capstone. All product and company names are trademarks™ or registered® trademarks of their respective holders.

Printed and bound in the USA. 6307

TABLE OF CONTENTS

CHAPTER 1
GHOSTLY GHOSTS 4

CHAPTER 2
CREEPY CRYPTIDS 14

CHAPTER 3
UFOS, ALIENS, AND
ABDUCTIONS 20

CHAPTER 4
MYSTERIES IN THE MAKING 28

CHAPTER 1

GHOSTLY GHOSTS

Some people say they can sense ghosts everywhere they go! Others have reported feeling the presence of ghosts while visiting certain places. If you've never felt a ghost, you might consider yourself lucky—or maybe you're hoping to visit a place that's full of them!

COMMON KINDS OF GHOSTS

Some people move on after death. Others like to stick around. Here are some of the most common types of ghosts.

- family members
- historical figures
- former residents of a home
- pets

DIFFERENT WORDS, DIFFERENT GHOSTS

- poltergeist—a ghost that can make noises and move things around
- specter—a ghost that haunts others
- wraith—a ghost that haunts without having died
- phantom—a ghost that can possess the living
- ghoul—an evil ghost
- spirit—an entity that can appear to the living

CLUES A GHOST MAY BE NEAR

- strange smells
- unexplained sounds
- flickering lights
- cold spots
- electronics losing power
- missing objects
- shadows
- odd dreams
- pets acting alarmed

FAMOUS FICTIONAL GHOSTS

- Casper the Friendly Ghost
- Beetlejuice
- Slimer from *Ghostbusters*
- the Vanishing Hitchhiker
- the *Flying Dutchman* and the ghost sailors in *Pirates of the Caribbean*
- Bloody Mary
- Moaning Myrtle from Harry Potter
- Danny Phantom
- the Headless Horseman

10 FAMOUS PLACES TO FIND GHOSTS

- Stanley Hotel—Estes Park, Colorado
- Farafra Desert—Egypt
- Whaley House—San Diego, California
- Zvikov Castle—Czechia
- Winchester Mystery House—San Jose, California
- Paris Catacombs—Paris, France
- Castle of Good Hope—Cape Town, South Africa
- Agrasen Ki Baoli step well—New Delhi, India
- Himeji Castle—Himeji, Hyogo, Japan
- Edinburgh Castle—Edinburgh, Scotland

FAMOUS GHOST STORIES

- *A Christmas Carol* by Charles Dickens
- *The Legend of Sleepy Hollow* by Washington Irving
- *The Ghost and Mrs. Muir* by R.A. Dick

SPOOKY ABILITIES

Some people claim they can communicate with ghosts. These abilities are called "sixth senses."

- clairvoyance—the ability to get information that isn't already known

- telepathy—the ability to communicate thoughts or ideas from one person's mind to another

- psychometry—the ability to discover information by touching objects

- remote viewing—using the mind to find distant or hidden objects

- astral projection—the ability to leave one's body to explore other places

HOW TO ATTRACT A GHOST

- Say their name—Beetlejuice, Bloody Mary, and other ghosts like to be invited.
- Show strong emotions—Some ghosts are drawn to anger, guilt, sorrow, or other emotions.
- Light a candle—This might get their attention!

HOW TO KEEP A GHOST AWAY

- Sprinkle salt near doorways or in circles.
- Ask them to leave.
- Hang an iron horseshoe or carry other iron objects with you.
- Cover mirrors.
- Remove any haunted items in the area.

GHOST-HUNTING TOOLS

Ghost hunters seek out spirits. There are special tools that help them find even shy ghosts.

- K2 meter—measures electromagnetic fields
- Mel meter—measures electromagnetic fields and temperature
- REM pod—creates an energy field
- SLS camera—captures 3D images
- paranormal trip wire—a motion detector for spirits
- thermal camera—detects infrared radiation

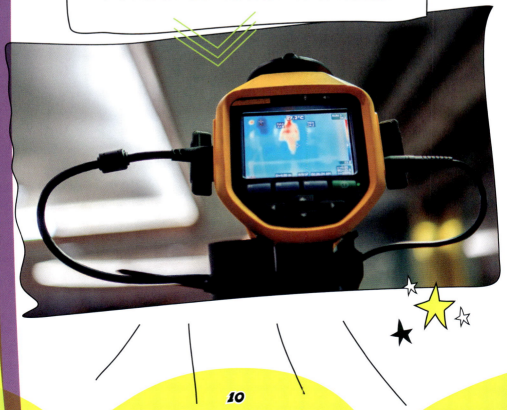

FAMOUS GHOST HUNTERS

- Ed and Lorraine Warren have been considered America's ghosts experts for more than 50 years and have inspired scary movies
- Harry Price was the first celebrity ghost hunter.
- Catherine Crowe investigated haunted houses and wrote a book about what she saw.
- Grant Wilson and Jason Hawes had a TV show called *Ghost Hunters* where they explored haunted places.

FAMOUS HAUNTED HOUSES

These places may not really be haunted, but they're great at tricking people into thinking they are!

- Disney's Haunted Mansion—Disneyland, Magic Kingdom, and Tokyo Disneyland
- Sacramento Scream Park—Sacramento, California
- Factory of Terror—Canton, Ohio
- Erebus—Pontiac, Michigan
- Cutting Edge Haunted House—Fort Worth, Texas

HAUNTED BODIES OF WATER

- Lake Lanier—one of the deadliest lakes in the United States, in Atlanta, Georgia
- Salt Island—wreck of the RMS *Rhone*, British Virgin Islands
- Red Sea—wreck of the SS *Thistlegorm*, Egypt
- Bride's Pool—river in Hong Kong, China, full of evil spirits
- MV *Joyita*—a ship that set sail from Samoa in October 1955 and was found abandoned five weeks later
- SS *Baychimo*—trapped in Alaskan ice in 1931 but has been seen drifting through Arctic waters ever since
- Devil's Pool—a waterfall in Queensland, Australia, haunted by a ghost

HAUNTED BATTLEFIELDS

- Gettysburg, Pennsylvania
- Passchendaele, Belgium
- Culloden, Inverness, Scotland
- Little Bighorn, Montana
- Volgograd, Russia
- Chickamauga, Georgia

PHANTOM SHIPS

These empty vessels drift along without a crew. They appear out of nowhere, then disappear without a trace.

- *Edmund Fitzgerald*—sank in Lake Superior near Michigan in 1975
- *Mary Celeste*—left New York in November 1872 and was found abandoned a month later
- *Flying Dutchman*—a legendary European ghost ship doomed to sail the ocean forever

CHAPTER 2

CREEPY CRYPTIDS

Cryptids are creatures people claim are real, but there's no proof of their existence. Or is there?

PROVE IT!

Cryptid hunters are always on the lookout for different kinds of proof that their favorite monsters are actually out there.

- footprints
- hair
- poop
- photos and videos
- eyewitness accounts

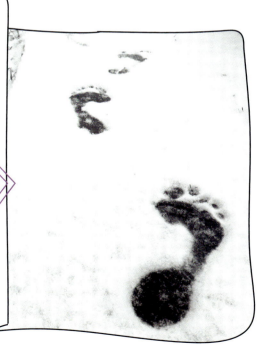

PROVEN CRYPTIDS

At one point, these animals were considered cryptids. Then, scientists found proof that they were real!

- 1798—platypus
- 1847—gorilla
- 1861—giant squid
- 1901—okapi
- 1910—Komodo dragon

CRYPTIDS AROUND THE WORLD

- Mongolian Death Worm—a giant worm in China and Mongolia's Gobi Desert
- Popobawa—a bat-like, shape-shifting demon that lives on Tanzania's Zanzibar islands
- Am Fear Liath Mòr—a big, gray man at the top of Scotland's second highest mountain
- Mokele-mbembe—a dinosaur-like creature in Africa's Congo River Basin
- Ahool—a bat-like creature in Indonesia
- Pombero—a small, human-like creature that protects Paraguay's forests
- Beast of Exmoor—a catlike creature in England
- Loch Ness Monster—a serpentlike creature in Scotland
- Bunyip—a man-eating creature that lives in the swamps of Australia

FURRY, FOUR-LEGGED CRYPTIDS

- Chupacabra—Puerto Rico
- Rougarou—Louisiana
- Manman Otter—Luoshi, China

GOATLIKE CRYPTIDS

- Goatman—Maryland
- Lake Worth Monster—Texas
- Pope Lick Monster—Kentucky

APELIKE CRYPTIDS

- Bigfoot—Pacific Northwest United States (also called Sasquatch)
- Yeti—Himalayan Mountains of Asia (also called the Abominable Snowman)
- Alamasty—central Asia
- Yowie—Australia
- Hibagon—Japan

AQUATIC CRYPTIDS

- Tahoe Tessie—a serpent or reptile in California and Nevada's Lake Tahoe
- Honey Island Swamp Monster—a part-alligator, part-chimp creature in Louisiana
- Ogopogo—a snake-like creature in Okanagan Lake, British Columbia, Canada
- Loveland Frogman—a humanoid frog in Little Miami River, Ohio
- Dobhar-chú—an otter-like animal in Ireland

CRYPTID MUSEUMS AROUND THE WORLD

- Ogoh-Ogoh Museum—Mengwi, Indonesia
- Museum of the Beast of Gevaudan—Saugues, France
- Museum Obscurum—Nykobing Falster, Denmark
- Icelandic Sea Monster Museum—Bíldudalur, Iceland
- Yokai Yashiki Museum—Miyoshi, Japan

CRYPTID MUSEUMS IN THE U.S.

- North American Bigfoot Center—Boring, Oregon
- China Flat Museum—Willow Creek, California
- Cryptozoology and Paranormal Museum—Littleton, North Carolina
- Expedition Bigfoot! The Sasquatch Museum—Blue Ridge, Georgia
- Flatwoods Monster Museum—Sutton, West Virginia
- Mothman Museum—Point Pleasant, West Virginia

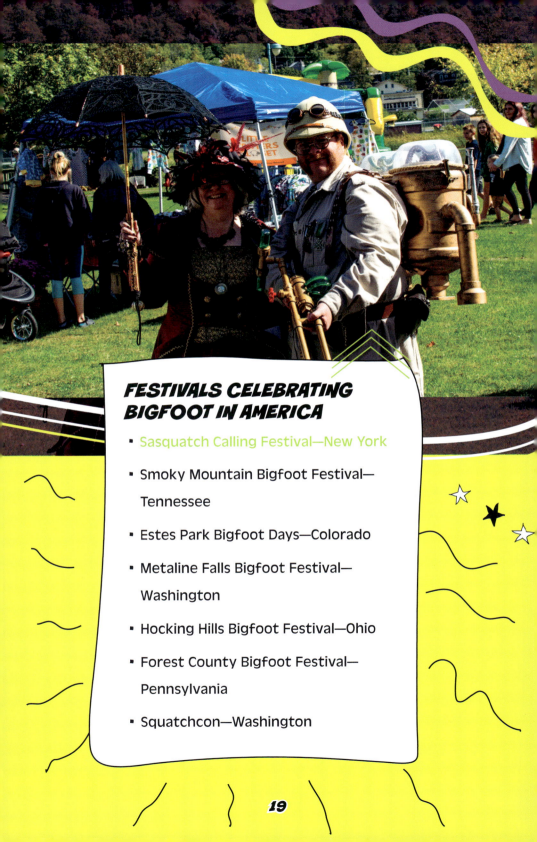

FESTIVALS CELEBRATING BIGFOOT IN AMERICA

- Sasquatch Calling Festival—New York
- Smoky Mountain Bigfoot Festival—Tennessee
- Estes Park Bigfoot Days—Colorado
- Metaline Falls Bigfoot Festival—Washington
- Hocking Hills Bigfoot Festival—Ohio
- Forest County Bigfoot Festival—Pennsylvania
- Squatchcon—Washington

CHAPTER 3

UFOS, ALIENS, AND ABDUCTIONS

Many people have claimed to see alien creatures. But not all of their descriptions are the same!

TYPES OF ALIENS

- little green men—short, green aliens with big black eyes and antennas

- Grays—the most-often reported beings, also called Zeta Reticulans (They look like very tall people with long limbs and big, black eyes.)

- Nordics—got their name because they resemble Scandinavian Earth people (They could be robots or clones.)

- Reptoids—lizard-like creatures

SUSPICIOUS ALIEN LOCATIONS

- Area 51—site of suspected UFO study near Las Vegas, Nevada
- Mountain Sphinx—a rock formation in Romania that was allegedly built by aliens
- Rendlesham Forest UFO Landing—site of a UFO incident in England
- Emilcin UFO Memorial—monument to an alien abduction in Poland

EARLY LITERARY MENTIONS OF ALIENS

- 100s CE—*A True Story* by Lucian of Samosata
- 1638—*The Man in the Moone* by Francis Godwin
- 1752—*Micromégas* by Voltaire
- 1897—*The War of the Worlds* by H.G. Wells

FICTIONAL ALIENS

- E.T.—from *E.T. the Extra-Terrestrial*
- Superman—from movies and comic books
- Stitch—from *Lilo & Stitch*
- The Boov—from the movie *Home,* based on the book *The True Meaning of Smekday*

UFO MUSEUMS

- The International UFO Museum and Research Center—Roswell, New Mexico
- Pine Bush UFO and Paranormal Museum—Orange County, New York
- The Xenobiology Museum—virtual
- Istanbul UFO Museum—Istanbul, Turkey

ALIEN CONVENTIONS

- AlienCon—Pasadena, Los Angeles, and Santa Clara, California; Baltimore, Maryland; Dallas, Texas
- Roswell UFO Festival—Roswell, New Mexico
- McMenamins UFO Fest—McMinnville, Oregon
- International UFO Congress—Laughlin, Nevada; Phoenix, Arizona

ANIMALS THAT LOOK LIKE ALIENS

- tarsier—look at those eyes!
- star-nosed mole—strange-shaped nose
- albino hedgehog—bright white with red eyes
- echidna—spiky body with a long, skinny nose
- common-Siamese soft-shelled turtle—smooth all over (Watch out—they bite!)
- aye-aye—long fingers, spooky eyes, and a piercing gaze

NEW TECH IN SEARCH OF ALIEN LIFE

- Square Kilometre Array—hundreds of radio telescopes in South Africa and Australia
- SETI—short for the Search for Extraterrestrial Intelligence, uses radio telescopes to scan the sky
- Vera C. Rubin Observatory—the world's largest camera, located in Chile
- artificial intelligence (AI)—looks for anomalies in space data

INVESTIGATIONS AND QUESTIONS

- Roswell crash—Did aliens land in New Mexico in 1947?

- Lubbock Lights—What were the weird lights over Texas in 1951?

- Shag Harbor—Did a UFO crash-land in Nova Scotia, Canada, in 1967?

- Belgian UFO Wave—Did people really see UFOs in 1989 and 1990?

- Rendlesham Forest Incident—Is there an explanation for the strange lights seen in England in 1980?

- Project Blue Book—Did the U.S. Air Force find UFOs between 1952 and 1969?

INFAMOUS ABDUCTIONS

- 1957—Brazilian Antonio Vilas-Boas claimed he was taken by 5-foot- (1.5-meter-) tall aliens.

- 1961—Barney and Betty Hill said they were abducted while driving home in New Hampshire.

- 1973—Calvin Parker and Charles Hickson claimed they were abducted and examined by aliens while on a fishing trip to Mississippi.

- 1975—Travis Walton, a forestry worker in Arizona, said he had been in a UFO.

TOP U.S. PLACES TO BE ABDUCTED BY ALIENS

Some places are UFO hotspots. These spots have the highest number of reported alien abductions.

- Lincoln County, Nevada—820.9 per 100,000 residents
- Arthur County, Nebraska—618.6 per 100,000 residents
- Alpine Valley, California—594.1 per 100,000 residents
- Hamilton County, New York—451.9 per 100,000 residents
- Dare County, North Carolina—371.4 per 100,000 residents

LAND HERE!

These places have rolled out the welcome mat for aliens.

- St. Paul, Alberta, Canada—The world's first UFO landing pad is located here.
- Spruce Pine, North Carolina—Willis Observatory is the only official UFO landing pad in the United States.
- Hurghada, Egypt—A work of art created by D.A.ST. Arteam looks like a UFO landed there. Maybe one will someday!

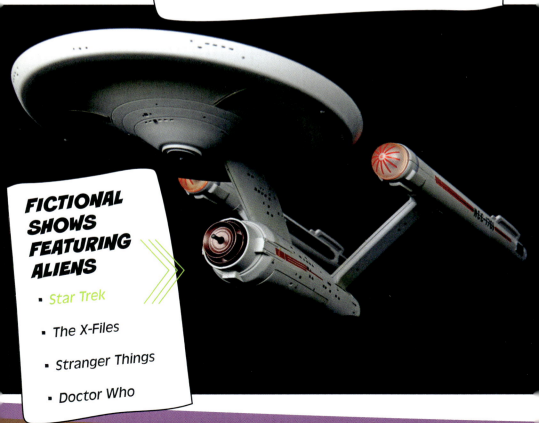

FICTIONAL SHOWS FEATURING ALIENS

- Star Trek
- The X-Files
- Stranger Things
- Doctor Who

GETTING ABDUCTED

Here's what some alien encounter survivors say they have experienced while in a UFO.

- capture—Aliens use high-tech equipment to capture people.
- warnings—Aliens deliver messages about the future.
- loss of time—People report time passing differently while with aliens.
- examination—Aliens conduct thorough examinations of people.

SHOWS AND MOVIES BASED ON REAL ALIEN ABDUCTIONS

- The Manhattan Alien Abduction
- Travis: The True Story of Travis Walton
- Linda Napolitano: The Alien Abduction of the Century

CHAPTER 4
MYSTERIES IN THE MAKING

There have been many unusual events over the years. Some are simply strange. Others are true mysteries!

UNEXPLAINED ENIGMAS

- Stonehenge—100 huge stones standing in a circle in England
- Nazca Lines—more than 1,000 enormous drawings of animals and plants etched into a desert in Peru
- Bermuda Triangle—an area of the Atlantic Ocean famous for mysterious disappearances
- Marfa Lights—bright orbs in the sky in Texas
- Plain of Jars—giant ancient jars on a plain in Laos

SIGNALS FROM SPACE

- Fast radio bursts—These radio pulses release about the same amount of energy as the Sun creates in a year; scientists don't know what causes them.

- A Sign in Space—A signal, crafted by SETI and sent from a European Space Agency orbiter in Mars, was beamed back to Earth as a test to model what a message from aliens might look like. People were challenged to decipher it.

- The Wow! signal—This radio signal came from the direction of the constellation Sagittarius in 1977.

MYSTERIOUS DISAPPEARANCES

- Roanoke Colony—an early North American settlement found deserted in 1590
- Flannan Isles Lighthouse—a Scottish lighthouse whose keepers disappeared in 1900
- Amelia Earhart—a pilot whose plane went missing over the Pacific Ocean in 1937
- D.B. Cooper—a hijacker who parachuted from a plane in 1971 and was never seen again
- Malaysian Airlines Flight 370—a passenger jet lost in 2014 with 239 people on board

GHOST TOWNS

People once called these places home. Today, they look like real towns, but nobody lives there. What happened?

- Centralia, Pennsylvania—abandoned due to a mine fire that has been burning beneath it since 1962
- Calico, California—a mining town abandoned in the 1890s when silver went down in value
- Bannack, Montana—abandoned after the gold rush ended and the train stopped running through the town
- Aten, Egypt—the Lost Golden City, abandoned 3,000 years ago near the city of Luxor
- Craco, Italy—a hillside town that was abandoned due to dangerous landslides

MORE INFO FANATIC BOOKS!

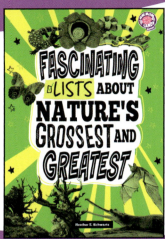

ABOUT THE AUTHOR

Heather E. Schwartz is an author, singer, and performance artist based in upstate New York. She loves writing because she loves learning new things and brainstorming creative ideas. A few sights she would like to see from this series include Cat Island, mammatus clouds, and Prada Marfa. She'd rather not experience spider rain! She lives with her husband and two kids, and their cats, Stampy and Squid.